FLASH
The Story of Me

FLASH
The Story of Me

NATALIE BRIGHT

CHRISTIE SHIPPY HEAD
LACY JOHNSTON PHOTOGRAPHY

All rights reserved. Copyright © Natalie Cline Bright (2018)

http://nataliebright.com

Published by NKB Books, LLC

EBook ISBN 978-09988101-4-0
Print ISBN 978-09988101-5-7

In collaboration with Christie Shippy Head
Edited by Denise McAllister
Photographs by Lacy Johnston Photography
Cover Design, Layout & Formatting by gessertbooks.com

DISCLAIMER

All rights reserved. No part of this book or this book as a whole may be used, reproduced or transmitted in any form or by any means, electronic, mechanical, photocopying, recording, scanning, or by an information storage and retrieval system, or transmitted by email without written permission from the author, except in the case of brief quotations embodied in critical articles and reviews. This book is for entertainment purposes only.

The views expressed are those of the author alone.

For any inquiries regarding this book, please email: natalie@nataliebright.com

DEDICATION

For horse lovers, everywhere. **NKB**

To Mom. Thanks for passing along the cowgirl spirit. **CSH**

CHAPTER 1
The Worst Day of My Life

Everybody calls me Flash. That is not my real name.

At birth, I was given the name Snake Creek Rooster. I am a registered Tennessee Walker, which means that I come from fancy bloodlines.

My instincts are natural to me because of my parents.

From the Tennessee Walker lineage, I have a smooth gait. I like people. I am loyal.

The spots on my legs and chest are unique. They are an important part of me. Because of my coloring, I am recognized with a Spotted Saddle Horse registry. I am double registered.

I lived in a pen and had a wonderful family. Life for me was simple and uneventful.

One day my entire world changed.

My family had to move. They could not take me with them. There was no place for me in their new home.

What would become of me?

Where would I go?

I had never been alone before.

CHAPTER 2
A Place for Me

There are people who offer shelter and food to homeless horses. I was one of the lucky ones to find such a place.

Dove Creek Ranch and Equine Rescue is a sanctuary of peace and beauty.

Nestled in a small valley, the ranch headquarters has several barns. I was led into a clean, roomy stall with an outdoor run.

Mr. Castillo, the ranch foreman, began working with me as soon as I arrived to determine my training level. He needed to know what I knew.

He rode me around a huge indoor arena. He introduced me to cows. We rode through the herd many times.

The people of Dove Creek were kind and patient. I liked my stall and the delicious food.

From my corral, I watched a herd of horses, goats, and burros graze under huge trees. They seemed so content.

I heard the wind rustle the leaves. I could smell the grass and the water that trickled in a nearby stream. The musical melody of a meadowlark or the *coo-coo* of a dove floated on the air above my head.

Even though I missed my family, I felt safe and secure here. Dove Creek Ranch was my new home.

CHAPTER 3
Running Free

One day Frank Castillo placed a halter on my head and took me out of my stall. He led me along the breezeway and out through the barn door. The warm sunshine felt good on my back.

We went through a gate and into a big pasture. He removed my halter and said, "Go on now."

I could not make my legs go at first. The pasture was so wide and long.

A few horses in the herd raised their heads to look my way. Some were more curious than others. They stopped grazing and walked slowly towards me.

Fields of green grass stretched for as far as I could see. I found myself surrounded by sun and sky. The smells of grass and of other horses filled my head. I breathed deeply.

I made new friends that day and I became part of a herd.

I ran free without fences.

CHAPTER 4
The Best Day of My Life

Frank brought me into the covered arena one afternoon. A lady with kind eyes waited there. She scratched my ears.

"I saw his picture on your website," she said. "I just had to meet him."

"He is good looking, Christie," said Frank. "But he can be a handful."

Frank told her this because sometimes I can be stubborn. I like to do things my own way.

"Maybe he is just super alert and scared," said Christie.

"This one can be a little wild," Frank said. "He is not easy to ride."

Christie stepped up into the saddle and we rode around the indoor arena several times. Frank opened the gates. She guided me outside through the pens. She steered me down the road to the ranch entrance. We came back again to the barn.

Christie hopped off my back and said, "I love his mind. I will take him."

Just like that I was adopted!

I left my family behind once again. I stepped into a trailer to travel to a new place I had never been before. Dove Creek Ranch saved me and had accepted me with open arms. I will never forget them, but I had a new adventure waiting.

CHAPTER 5
I am Adopted!

Christie loaded me in her trailer and took me home. I left behind my family again and traveled to somewhere I'd never been before.

If I had known then what Christie had in store for me, I might have put up a much bigger fight. The only thing this gal knows is work.

We trained together almost every day.

On some days, I didn't want to do it. Who does she think she is making me work day in and day out? We rode around in circles, back and forth along the road. It was endless.

I must admit I started to like it though. I liked spending time with Christie. Days with a human are so very different than the time I grazed with a herd of horses. People make me think. Christie kept my mind occupied and helped me to learn new things.

I am smart and at last I understood what she wanted. I found my stride. My gaited stride felt good and natural.

There was only one problem though. Noise.

I hated noise. Strange, sudden sounds did not make sense to me. What could those odd sounds be? I just knew it was going to be horrible and hurt me.

Christie said, "Flash, you have to learn how to stay calm. Noises aren't going to hurt you. I promise."

Sometimes, I could not stop myself.

I twitch and jerk my head at strange noises. The only solution in Christie's mind—more work.

We trained. And we trained some more.

Christie had something planned for us. At the time, I did not understand why she pushed me so hard. Even though I enjoyed our time together, I had no idea what she had in mind.

CHAPTER 6
Being Headstrong

Sometimes I can be naughty.

It makes me crazy to have to do something when I don't want to. I don't know why I have such a stubborn streak, but I do.

When Christie backs up the trailer and I don't know where we're going, I decide that I'm not going. I act horrible. I run across the corral and kick up my heels.

One day I ran into a panel and bent it just because I didn't want to get in the trailer. Christie was very angry. I could tell I had made her unhappy.

What happened next shocked me.

Christie loaded my corral mates: Bya, Wildfire, Roscoe, and Albert. They drove off. Without me! Can you believe it?

She left me.

She left me standing in the corral by myself. The nerve of my human.

Where did they go? Would they ever come back? I just knew I'd never see them again. That's the day I decided acting nice was a lot easier than acting naughty.

One morning Christie saddled me, and then loaded Bya with me into the trailer. Christie's daughter Audrey came too. We traveled until we came to a deep canyon. Christie drove slowly down into the canyon on a winding road, which hugged the cliff's edge. The walls of the canyon were steep and went straight up to the sky. We parked on a gravel space next to the paved road. A dirt path led into the junipers and mesquite trees.

At the time, I had no idea where the path would lead. Traveling down that trail would change my life forever.

Little did I know how that path and my new family would give my life purpose again.

CHAPTER 7
The Deep Canyon

We unloaded next to the paved road that had taken us into the deep canyon. We followed a hard-packed footpath. The dirt trail turned to hard rocks. Christie got off my back and led me over and around the rocky ledge. She got back on and we kept going.

We crossed a narrow land bridge. There was a deep gorge on both sides. Bya went across with no trouble. I hesitated at first. If she could do it, I could too.

After a mile of riding and walking, we emerged from a clump of mesquite trees and the view took my breath away. I could see for miles along a deep canyon. The banded walls stretched straight up to the flat prairie. A small stream twisted and turned along the canyon's bottom.

Christie had a flag with her. With stripes and a star, it was the flag of my state. She guided me down a trail that ran next to the edge of the canyon. Then she guided me back to the same starting point. We walked and loped this trail over and over many times.

She had me stand at the starting spot again. I sensed this time was going to be different. She pointed me straight towards the trail and settled her seat in the saddle. She held the flag with her right hand, and gripped my reins with her left. She leaned forward in the saddle, lifted the reins ever so slightly, and squeezed her legs. She shouted, "Hey!"

I worked myself up to a fast trot. That's not what she wanted.

We tried again. Christie wanted me to run.

We trailered out to the canyon many times after that day and worked on that rim trail until I finally understood the signal to run.

I knew we'd run. I could hardly wait. I knew that I could run as fast as the wind. But I had to stand perfectly still for a few minutes until Christie told me to go. That was the hardest part, standing still.

One day it all became perfectly clear to me. The training, the long days of work, and the effort to help me overcome my fear of noises.

I had a job to do, and it was an important one at that.

CHAPTER 8
Show Time

One evening, just before sunset, I looked down into the canyon and saw people. Lots of people. All eyes were turned up towards me and Christie as we stood on our rim trail.

There was music, too. But the noise didn't bother me. I had learned to trust my new owner. I knew that she would never let anything hurt me.

The other rider had a two-way radio, and she asked if we were ready. "Stage director says go," she said.

Christie nodded her head.

"Hey!", she shouted.

I gave it all I had. I could feel the power in my back leg muscles, and I stretched out my front legs as far as I could. With all of the power I had, I stretched and ran.

The crowd went wild with shouts and clapping. The noise didn't bother me.

I did my job perfectly.

Really, I did. I had a total understanding of what was expected of me.

The purpose of the training had all led up to this one moment— when I would run the rim trail with a Texas flag billowing behind us.

That night when Christie gave me fresh hay and filled my water trough, she hugged my neck. She talked softly to me, like she often does.

"You are a good boy, Flash," she said. "I am so proud of you."

CHAPTER 9
This Isn't the End

That summer we worked hard. Every day of the week, except for Mondays, we trailered up the winding road to the gravel spot and parked. We unloaded and walked the mile-long dirt path to the rim trail. We ran, with the state flag blowing behind us. We trailered back down into the deep canyon to the amphitheatre stage. I stood on my marks every time. The noise of the crowd, the fireworks, and the loud music did not bother me any longer.

I had a job to do. I became a star that summer.

The funny thing about life is that it is always changing. Just when I feel comfortable and know my place in this world, things change. The life you had before can be totally different from the life you have now.

That summer was demanding work and very hot, but I had a job to do and I did it.

I have learned that if you set your mind to it, you can achieve anything.

THE END

UP FOR DISCUSSION

- Would you have the patience to train a horse? Why or Why not?

- What part of Flash's story do you like the best?

- What have you been afraid of that someone helped you overcome?

- If you could take Flash home for the weekend, what would you do?

- Wanted: A New friend for Flash. What kind of animal friend would you find for Flash? Why?

- If you could find Flash a new job, what would you ask him to do?

- If you could talk to animals, what would you say to Flash?

- Flash is ready for a vacation. Where would you take him? Why?

- What do you think Flash is doing now that his job at the outdoor musical has ended?

- How would the story change if Flash could travel to the moon? What kind of job could Flash do in outerspace?

CONTRIBUTORS

Natalie Cline Bright, is the author of the *Trouble in Texas* series for middle grades, as well as the *Rescue Animal Series* which sheds light on the people who are dedicated to giving horses a second chance. Her articles and short stories have appeared in numerous publications. Download Flash coloring pages and sign up for a FREE eNewsletter at her website http://nataliebright.com

Christie Shippy Head, Owner/Trainer, is a horse loving, elementary school music teacher who has been blessed to raise her family in the Texas Panhandle. Over several summers, she worked as the Head Wrangler for the musical drama TEXAS, supervised a crew of wranglers, and trained the livestock that became a part of the cast. She adopted Flash and trained him to "ride the rim". She has been involved with horses from a young age and loves everything to do with these magnificent creatures. Her passions include playing the piano, sharing her love of music and horses with others, and spending time with her family.

Lacy Johnston, Photographer, works as a professional real estate photographer for Coldwell Banker in Amarillo. She also maintains an extensive client list and enjoys photographing weddings, family events, and spotted horses. In her spare time she loves being outdoors with her husband.

Denise McAllister, Editor, has been writing stories since she was 10 years old. A business editor for the past 20+ years, she edits publications and websites for global corporations in Austria, Finland, and the U.S. Although she works on beautiful Hilton Head Island, SC as a communications coordinator/editor, Denise's heart is drawn to horses and anything Western. She writes contemporary Western fiction and nonfiction, book reviews, and has edited books for members of the Western Writers of America organization.

Phillip Gessert, Graphic Design and Formatting, lent his talent to the book cover and layout design. http://www.gessertbooks.com

Thanks to Kirsti Kasch and Molly McKnight for providing the questions; UP FOR DISCUSSION. For more educator activity guidelines, go to https://nataliebright.com

Special thanks to Dove Creek Equine Rescue for introducing Flash to Christie and for graciously allowing us to photograph their facility. Find out more about the work they do and how you can sponsor a well-deserving horse by going to their website.

https://www.dovecreekequinerescue.org/

CONNECT WITH
us Online!

- Follow Flash on Instagram:
  https://www.instagram.com/flashtherescuehorse

FIND NATALIE
online here

- Website: https://www.nataliebright.com
- Twitter: https://twitter.com/natNKB
- Instagram: https://wwwinstagram.com/natsgrams
- Pinterest: https://www.pinterest.com/natbright
- Facebook: https://www.facebook.com/nataliebrightauthor
- LinkedIn: https://www.linkedin.com/in/natalie-bright-b451472b

Thank you for sharing the story of Flash with your emerging readers. Help other readers find this book by recommending it to your family, friends, educators, book clubs, and readers' groups. If you love the story of Flash, please let others know by posting an online review.

Need a program for your group or club? Contact information and program synopsis can be found on Natalie's website.

www.ingramcontent.com/pod-product-compliance
Lightning Source LLC
Chambersburg PA
CBHW051555010526
44118CB00022B/2717